The Story Begins

Several years ago, people realised that they could use their computers to do business. New companies appeared, selling books, records, clothing and many other items over the Internet.

Until recently, people had to travel to towns and cities to go shopping. Some people ordered over the telephone. Others shopped using a catalogue. However, none of these ways was as exciting as the new way of shopping over the Internet.

As we enter the new millennium, the Internet is set to revolutionise how we live our lives – how we communicate, how we do business and how we manage our time. This is the story of the Internet, and how we can use it to buy the things we need today.

beeb.com and Ladybird have joined together to help make sense of this for you.

'How it works'

SHOPPING ON THE INTERNET

by CHAS BAYFIELD, JIM BOLTON and LESLEY HENRY

with illustrations by M. THOMAS, T. CONNELL,
J. SAYER and R. PEARMAN

Published by BBC Worldwide Limited
BBC Worldwide Woodlands 80 Wood Lane London W12 OTT
© beeb Ventures Limited, MM   Printed in Italy

0 563 53779 5

The first 'information superhighway'

People have been doing business for thousands of years. From around 200BC until the 14th century people traded ivory, precious stones, glass and gold from the west with furs, ceramics, jade and silk from the east. The merchants used an ancient thoroughfare which stretched between the steppes of European Russia through the vast Mongol lands of Asia and on to China. This was the Silk Road.

The Silk Road was as much a meeting place as it was a trade route. Think of it as a giant river of ideas, information and merchandise, fed by many smaller tributaries. For this reason, the Silk Road has been called the Internet of its day. The original traders faced dangers and perils that hardly bear thinking about. Today's Internet users face much lesser hardships, but using the Internet is still not free from hazards. This book will help you understand how you can use the Internet to buy things safely.

Before we begin though, it is important to learn about the people whose discoveries and achievements have pioneered computing and the Internet.

A camel train on the Silk Road

The first computers

The first programmable computing device was called the Difference Engine. It was the idea of an Englishman called Charles Babbage. Babbage began building his Difference Engine in 1823, but it was never completed during his lifetime. Historians believe Babbage was so ahead of his time that the technology of the day was not reliable enough for him to finish building his computer! You may be interested to know that there is a working model of the Difference Engine in the Science Museum in London.

One of the first modern computers was Colossus, designed by Alan Turing and his fellow engineers for the British army in 1943. Colossus played an important role in breaking codes used by the German army in World War II.

In 1980 another Englishman, Clive Sinclair, produced the ZX80, a computer that you could build yourself from a kit. It was cheap and basic, but very popular. The personal computer was born.

The first personal computer, or PC, to look like the PCs we use today was introduced in August 1981 by an American company called International Business Machines. It was called the IBM 5150.

Babbage and his Difference Engine

Life before e-mail

As early as 1874, a Frenchman named Emile Baudot developed a machine that could send letters and numbers along wires. The invention of teleprinters soon followed and 'Telex' was used extensively by businesses from the 1920s to the 1980s. Thanks to these inventions, people were able to use machines to send each other written messages long before they had computers.

It is easy to think of e-mail as quite a recent invention. Scientists, however, have been using e-mail for many years. The first e-mail message was sent by Professor Leonard Kleinrock in Los Angeles to a colleague at Stanford University back in October 1969. His colleague's computer promptly crashed!

In its simplest form, e-mail is an electronic message sent between computers that are linked together in a network. But what is a computer network? We will read later of how computers talk to one another.

During the 1960s, the countries in the West, such as Britain and America, were suspicious of the countries in the East, such as Russia and parts of Germany. This was known as the Cold War. America wanted to find a way of allowing people to keep in touch with one another in the event of a nuclear war. However, the development of a network of computers that are linked up to one another had begun anyway, and would probably have continued even if there had been no Cold War.

How e-mail works

Jane Jones
janejones@beeb.net)
sends an e-mail to
John Smith
hnsmith@hotmail.com)

Mailserver
for
hotmail.com

The hotmail.com
mailserver checks
the address
(like the address
on an envelope)
and forwards
it on to
johnsmith@hotmail.com

E-mail arrives at
johnsmith@hotmail.com

E-mail arrives at
janejones@beeb.net

Mailserver
for
beeb.net

The mailserver
for beeb.net
checks the address
and forwards
it on to
janejones@beeb.net

johnsmith@hotmail.com
replies to
janejones@beeb.net

The Fathers of the Internet

In the 1960s, an American scientist called Douglas Engelbart imagined people sitting in front of screens, 'flying around' and connecting with one another in an information space. Here ideas could be created and stored quickly and simply. This 'information space' would later be known as cyberspace.

By the autumn of 1968, Engelbart had found a way of letting computers talk to one another in a network. He called this system oNLine. That's why today, when people are using the Internet, it is called being online. If you use a mouse on your computer, you have Engelbart to thank, for he invented that too!

In 1969, America's Advanced Research Projects Agency, or ARPA, asked Engelbart to link a computer at Stanford University in California with three other computers in the western United States. This link would be called the ARPANET, the first computer network.

By 1974, two more Americans, Bob Kahn and Vint Cerf, had found a way of linking the ARPANET with another network. The name 'Internet' came from the way it allowed people to have inter-network conversations.

In 1977, American Dennis Hayes invented a small box that could take written text from a computer and send it along telephone wires (**mod**ulating). The box could also translate signals coming through a phone line into text again (**dem**odulating). Hayes called his box a 'modem'. It was Hayes' modem that finally prepared the way for the online and Internet industries we know today.

The first successful Internet connection

The Internet explained

The Internet, or 'Net' as it is more commonly known, is a network of networks. It is made up of computers and cables. Cerf and Kahn worked out how you could use computers and cables to send little packets of information between networks.

Think of a packet as a bit like a postcard with a simple address on it. If you put the right address on a packet, and give it to any computer that is connected as part of the Internet, each computer will work out which cable to send it down next so that it will reach its destination.

When you type in an Internet address and hit the send button, your packet of information shoots through cables until it reaches its destination – the web site that you wish to look at. The Internet delivers packets anywhere in the world, normally in well under a second.

The work of men like Cerf, Kahn and Engelbart impressed a young English scientist, Tim Berners-Lee. Berners-Lee created a simple way of sending and retrieving information over the Internet. He called this the 'Hyper Text Transfer Protocol'. That is why most Internet addresses have the letters 'http' in front of them.

An Internet network

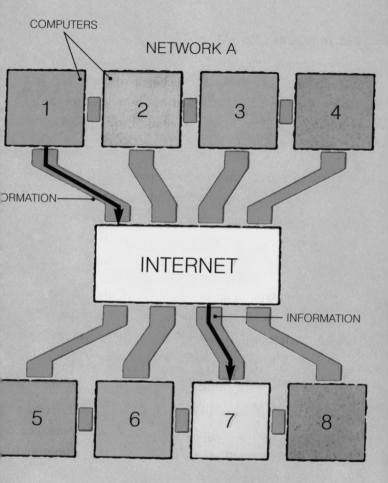

COMPUTERS

NETWORK A

1 2 3 4

INFORMATION

INTERNET

INFORMATION

5 6 7 8

NETWORK B

THIS DIAGRAM EXPLAINS HOW INFORMATION CAN BE SENT
FROM COMPUTER 1 ON NETWORK A VIA THE INTERNET TO
COMPUTER 7 ON NETWORK B.

The Father of the World Wide Web

On the Internet, which is a vast network of computers, you can communicate with other people using e-mail and newsgroups. The Web is made up of the words and images contained within the Internet. On the Web, connections are hypertext links: those strings of letters beginning with 'http'. These links travel electronically through the cables and wires that link computers. These 'http' addresses help you navigate easily from one site to another. So, 'http://www' is the prefix used by most web sites on the Internet.

Berners-Lee saw the packets of information on the Internet as locations on a giant web. By using http, Internet addresses could be simplified (they all would begin 'http') and they could be speedily retrieved and called up on-screen for viewing. Berners-Lee called these locations on the Internet 'web sites'. The World Wide Web had been born.

In 1991, America's High Performance Computing Act provided money for further research into computing and for improving the framework, or 'infrastructure' of the Internet. The Internet was about to become the 'Information Superhighway'.

By the end of 1992, there were just 50 web sites – there are now many thousands of web sites. On the opposite page, you will see some 'pages' from Tim Berners-Lee's web site in 1993. Notice how plain it is. Back then, web sites were almost all made up of text instead of pictures.

14   **Some early Berners-Lee web pages**

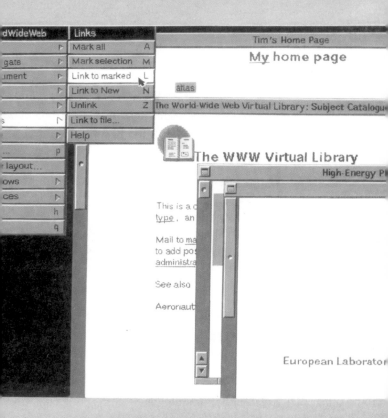

The equipment you will need

There are several important pieces of equipment which are needed before you can gain access to the Internet. To make it easier for you, most computer shops sell them together.

First, of course, you need a computer. You will also need a monitor. This is a box with a screen. You will need a keyboard and a mouse. The mouse is usually attached to the keyboard with a cable, or, on some computers, it is a special key on the keyboard. Lastly, you need a modem. This may be a small box, one end of which is plugged into a telephone socket, the other end of which is attached to the computer. Some modems are inside the computer already.

By using the Internet, all you are doing is typing letters or numbers into a computer, rather than dialling numbers into a phone. The modem changes the typed information into code before it begins its journey down the phone line. At the other end, another modem changes the code back to typed information again. Modems will let you send and retrieve pictures over the Internet, too.

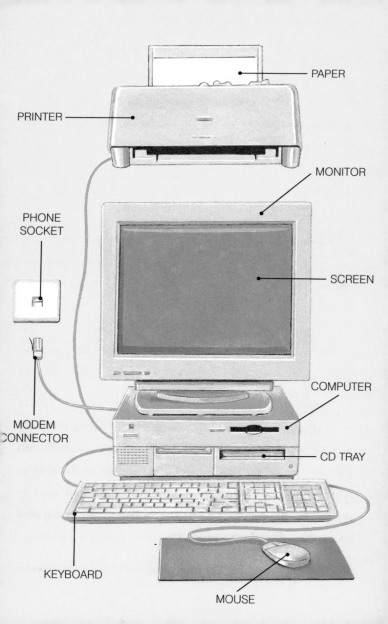

PAPER

PRINTER

PHONE
SOCKET

MONITOR

SCREEN

MODEM
CONNECTOR

COMPUTER

CD TRAY

KEYBOARD

MOUSE

Using your computer

Once you have wired up your computer correctly, it's time to switch it on. Don't worry, you don't need to be able to type well or to understand the science of computers to use the Internet. The companies behind the Internet have made it very easy for both children and adults to use.

You will notice a small arrow which moves when you move the mouse. You can use this to tell the computer where you wish to type information. Usually, the instructions on the screen tell you where to type. If the instruction on screen is to 'click here', simply move the mouse so the arrow is over the place where you wish to click. Then press your finger down on the mouse. Click!

Typing information into a computer is very much like using a typewriter. Although, if you make a mistake, you can use the delete key. Unlike a shop, you don't have to worry about closing time – online shops are always open! Moreover, you don't have to worry about a queue of people behind you while you are making a purchase.

Using the mouse

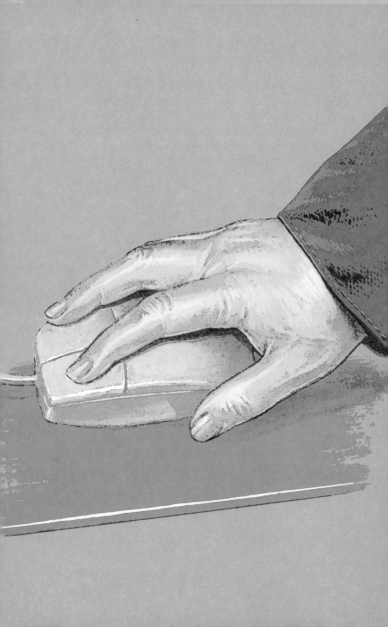

Gaining access to the Internet

The companies that provide people with Internet access are called Internet service providers, or ISPs. You may have heard of some of the bigger ISPs – Freeserve, BT, AOL and beeb.net. Each ISP has its own way of charging money. It is worth checking which ISP would best suit your needs depending on the amount of time you wish to spend online. ISPs also vary in the level of service they provide. This is because the ISP's server, which is the computer it uses to connect all its subscribers to the Internet, can only handle a certain number of users at one time. When it reaches that number the connection slows down, just like traffic slows down on a busy road.

Once you have chosen your ISP, you will need one of its compact discs to connect your computer to its service. Although it may look the same, this isn't a CD that plays music or tells a story, it is a CD that talks in a special language to your computer. This is called a CD ROM. The CD ROM should be placed in the special CD ROM tray in the computer. It will come with instructions on how to use it.

Because the Internet involves using your telephone line, your telephone will transmit an 'engaged' signal, should people call you while you are online. Some people arrange for a second telephone line for their home if they are going to use the Internet a lot. Most telephone companies have special offers which enable you to install a second line for using the Internet.

Your ISP will also provide you with an e-mail account. Often, they will give you one or more e-mail addresses. beeb.net, for example will give you as many e-mail addresses as you wish. With many ISPs, you can read and send e-mail from any computer in the world that has Internet access.

Placing the CD ROM into the CD ROM tray

Finding a web site

Once you have followed the instructions of your ISP, a small graphic shape will appear on your screen when you switch your computer on. This is called an 'icon'. Click on this icon and you will be connected to an Internet browser. Internet browsers allow you to view anything on the World Wide Web. Browsers are regularly improved and updated. Any web site will look and work best with an up-to-date browser. The two main browsers are Netscape Navigator and Internet Explorer. Once you have clicked on the icon, your modem dials up a number which allows you access into the Internet. You are online, or to give it another name, 'wired'.

Sometimes you know exactly the Internet address you want. This usually begins with http://www. Use your mouse to move the arrow on the screen until it is over the box where you can type in the address you want: http://www.beeb.com for example. Once you have typed in the correct address, just press the return key. This is the key on the right of your keyboard with an arrow pointing down and left. Within a few moments, the web site should appear on your screen. Sometimes you might see an 'Error' message at this point instead of your site. This usually happens when you have typed in the address incorrectly or when there is something wrong with the site you are trying to connect to. Try re-entering the address making sure you enter it with all the correct full stops, spaces or slashes – even the smallest mistake means you won't reach the correct site!

If you want information about a certain subject, you can use a 'search engine'. Search engines literally search the World Wide Web for information that matches the information you are looking for.

The Internet address box

| ack | Forward | Reload | Home | Search | Favorites | Images | Print | Security | Stop |

http://www.beeb.com/

Using a search engine

Search engines are an easy way of finding the web site you need. There are two types of search engines: web crawlers and directories. Web crawlers, such as Alta Vista and Google, are run automatically by machines. These web crawlers send out little electronic 'spiders' that scout the Internet looking for information on web sites. They then file this information on a system like a vast card index box. Other companies, such as Yahoo, operate directories which are managed by men and women who look at pages on the Web. They then decide how to categorise them. This means there is more human judgement involved than there is with web crawlers.

Both web crawlers and directories have a box on the screen in which you may type the key words you wish to look up, for example, 'dishwashers'. The search engine will then search the Web for any mention of dishwashers. Web crawlers list as many sites as the spiders can find containing this word. Directories search through a list of web site descriptions that the owners of the sites have written.

A list of web sites that contain information about dishwashers will appear on screen. Just click on the one that you think will be most useful and you will be taken to the web site you have chosen. You are almost ready to begin shopping on the Internet.

Forward Reload Home Search Favorites Print Security Stop

Bookmarks Netsite /search.gw?search=dishwashers

rch

onalize | Check Email

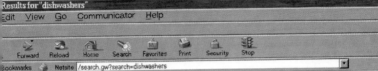

 BBC good **homes**

Web Search • Category Search • News Search • Photo Search • Audio/Video Search

earch Web Sites:

ishwashers   Search   Search Home • Help
                                                                           Advanced Search

op 10 Web Site Results for: **dishwashers**

| Home Appliances CLICK HERE! |

What a web site looks like

On the opposite page is a web page. It is part of the BBC's Good Homes web site. It is the **Good Homes home page** – the important page that links you to all the other pages on the site.

At the top of the page is a **banner ad.** This is an advertisement for another company. This company has paid money to place its advertisement here, just as it would pay to place it in a newspaper or magazine. Click on the banner ad and you will be taken to the advertiser's web site.

There are photos on the page. These are called JPEGs (named after the Joint Photographic Experts Group). JPEGs are specially designed to appear on your screen quickly. Any text graphics on the page, such as logos are called GIFs (Graphics Interchange Format). Throughout the page are **links**. These link you to another page on the Web. Text links are usually underlined, or appear in a different colour. Since the days of Tim Berners-Lee's early web pages, generally these have been blue. You can tell if a picture or a piece of text is a link by moving the arrow over it with your mouse. If the arrow changes into a pointing finger, it is a link. Click the mouse to see where the link will take you.

Also on the page is a **drop down box.** This is like a menu, and can be used to provide a choice of links to help you find what you want.

A typical home page

File   Edit   View   Go   Communicator   Help

Back   Forward   Reload   Home   Search   Favorites   Print   Security   Stop

Bookmarks   Netsite   http://www.goodhomes.beeb.com/index.shtml

 good **homes** **SHOPPING**GUIDE

be inspired...

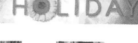 HOLIDAY

 beeb.com

  cooking/dining bathing sleeping outdoor living

advice

webclub

good homes magazine

special offers

prizes and treats

BBC

The first 'e-tailers'

The first companies selling their goods and services on the Internet date from the mid 1990s. Perhaps the best known of these 'e-tailers' is Amazon.

Amazon was set up in Seattle, in America, in 1995 by a young businessman called Jeff Bezos. The company concentrated on good service and low prices. Originally, Amazon sold books, but today it sells many goods and services.

Today, there are many online shops (or 'e-tailers'). Some, like Amazon, only exist on the Internet. Others are names that we recognise from the high street. Shops such as WH Smith and Marks and Spencer are now online as well as in our towns and cities. These companies realised that shopping on the Internet would be far more convenient for many people.

There are many reasons for choosing to shop on the Internet. You can shop whenever you wish – the Internet never closes! You can read information before you buy more complicated items like holidays, cars or electrical goods; you can compare the price of the same item at a range of different online shops to find the best price; and you can have the goods delivered directly to your home, usually within a couple of days. In fact, it can be much easier to buy things over the Internet than it is to spend a day wandering along the high street.

Some of the things you can buy online

Choosing your online purchase

Many online shopping guides, including beeb.com, allow you to compare the price of the same product at a number of different e-tailers. This can be especially useful if you're looking for the lowest price or quickest delivery.

To compare prices, most sites first offer you a choice of categories to choose from, such as books or CDs. Once you have made your selection, type in the product or manufacturer that you're looking for and click on the search button. Within a few seconds your results will be returned with details of the online shops, their prices and delivery times.

However, some online shops may not have included all their charges within their prices, charges such as delivery costs or VAT. Make sure that you are aware of the final price that will be charged to your credit card when you are at the checkout.

Comparing prices online is quick because you can compare the prices from lots of different online shops simultaneously. But remember, you are only seeing prices for a selection of e-tailers. That is not to say that any price displayed cannot be beaten elsewhere on the Internet.

Shopping basket

The first thing we all do when we walk into a shop on the high street is to pick up a basket or trolley. Shopping online is just the same – e-tailers use an icon or picture of a shopping basket in which to put the items that you wish to buy. Whenever you see a product that you want to buy, simply click on it to add the product to your individual shopping basket. Don't worry! You can always change your mind later and remove items from your shopping basket. Remember, until you go to the checkout or type in your credit card number you are not spending any money, so it's safe to try it out and see what happens.

Search | Choosing | Jobs | Designing | You &

Gardeners' World » Choosing plants and products

Akebia quinata
Chocolate vine

now buy it with beeb.com

Search completed

Reseller	Description	Location	Delivery charge	Total cost	
				£11.90	buy it
				£15.51	buy it
				£12.94	buy it

Paying for and receiving your goods

At the checkout

Once you have decided on the purchases you would like to make, it's time to go and pay for them. At this point in your journey you should still be able to discard any items that you don't want, as you have not paid for them. Just like any shopping checkout or till, all the products are added up to give you a final bill.

Check any additions to your final total, such as postage and packing or VAT, to make sure you know exactly how much you are spending, and if it is not clear what you are being charged just leave the site.

To make your purchase, just enter the number from your credit card or debit card and follow the instructions on the screen.

Delivery

Delivery time depends on what product you buy, the availability of the stock and what time of day you complete your order. Some shops can deliver books or CDs within 24 hours, while others may take slightly longer, particularly if they need to come from abroad. Once you have made your purchase, most sites send an e-mail to confirm your order and the delivery date. Check the delivery date before you buy and make a note of any order reference you are given.

Refunds

If you are not satisfied with the goods you have bought then let the e-tailer know – e-mail or telephone them. Respectable online shops are more than happy to help you, as they value your custom and may even refund the return postage.

Guarantees

Many good online shops are part of the Which? Web Trader scheme. These e-tailers follow the Which? Code of Practice that aims to protect us while we shop online. For example, all beeb.com's partners are members of Which? or a similar scheme and they follow beeb.com's trading standards.

All these are available on the Internet

Keeping the Internet safe

Credit cards and secure servers

Using credit cards on the Web should be every bit as safe as giving your credit card details over the phone or buying products by mail order.

Reputable online e-tailers use a technology called SSL (Secure Sockets Layer). This technology changes any information that you supply into code. This is called 'encryption'. Encryption makes it virtually impossible for any other user to read it. Most e-tailers who use SSL will display a key or padlock symbol in the bottom right-hand corner of your screen. Check in their 'privacy policy' to see if they use SSL.

If you are connected to a site where the symbol isn't shown or appears or to be broken, it may be that they have no reason to take credit card payments. If they do take credit cards and make no mention of SSL anywhere on their site, then you cannot trust the site to keep your information a secret. In this case, it is not advisable to type in your credit card number or personal details.

To make online shopping even safer, many credit card companies will not charge you if somebody uses your credit card details against your wishes. Why not check to see whether your credit card company is one of these?

Your personal information

Many of us hand over personal information such as our name, address and credit card details when we make purchases or order through a catalogue. It is no different when we shop online. Most online shops follow the relevant European Union data protection legislation to ensure our details are kept safe. Make sure you are happy with the Privacy Policy of any e-tailer you visit before you hand over any personal information. Respectable e-tailers will never pass on any of your personal information without your permission to do so.

Cookies

When you visit a web site, the site can collect and store small bits of information about you. These pieces of information are called 'cookies'. They are stored on your computer and carry details from when you visited that site. (Cookies do not harm your computer in any way). Should you revisit the web site, your computer will send this helpful information back to the site automatically. For example, an online bookstore might use a cookie to record the authors and titles of books you may have ordered from them before. When you return to the online bookstore, your computer lets the bookstore's site read the cookie. The site might then recommend a list of books by the same authors, or books on similar topics, and show you that list. No one really knows where the name cookie came from!

When you visit a web site, the site can tell which ISP you are using, what site you last visited and which browser you are using. Don't worry, the site has no way of knowing your name, e-mail address, postal address, or other information about you – unless you explicitly provide that information.

The information that cookies supply gives online shops a greater understanding of you and your interests. That way they can recommend products, services and promotions that they feel would be of interest to you. Personal information that you give by entering competitions or signing up to clubs or special e-mail services can also provide web site owners with more information about your likes and dislikes.

How cookies work

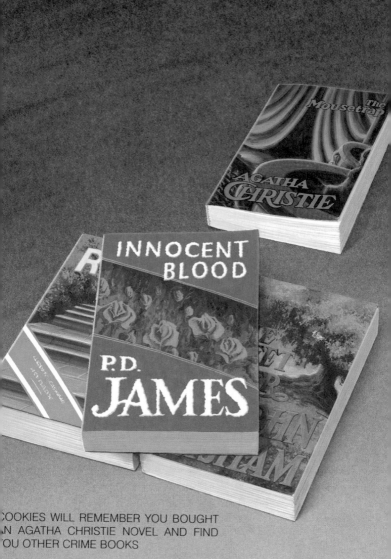

COOKIES WILL REMEMBER YOU BOUGHT
AN AGATHA CHRISTIE NOVEL AND FIND
YOU OTHER CRIME BOOKS

Portals

Some Internet retailers specialise in one particular area, such as hmv.co.uk for music or The First Resort for travel. There are also sites that offer a wider range of goods. For example, Amazon sells books, music, videos, PCs and software.

Some shopping sites are called 'portals'. They bring together a number of different web sites in one place so that it is more convenient for people – they are just like department stores online.

Some of these portals simply list all the sites where you can buy particular goods or services, while others allow you to compare prices across a range of different online shops.

beeb.com is a shopping portal. The sites on beeb.com are all named after well-known BBC television programmes and magazines, for example, Top of the Pops. Top of the Pops uses its years of experience as the nation's favourite popular music show to give you impartial reviews on more than forty thousand bands. You may also view a list of records by one artist and listen to sound clips from over one million songs. Should you wish to buy a CD, the Top of the Pops page will link you to a number of online shops that sell music – BOL.com, for example.

Other web sites on beeb.com are Good Homes, Gardeners' World, Top Gear, Holiday, BBC Music, Radio Times and All About Eve. All these sites offer the user expert advice, reviews, information and links to web sites where a purchase can be made. In line with the BBC's policy on impartiality, beeb.com strives to be impartial and you are always given a choice of e-tailers from which to shop.

beeb.com was built on five principles: to be clear and easy to understand, to provide a safe Internet shopping environment, to protect your personal information, to give impartial advice and to be always accessible.

The beeb.com site

Back   Forward   Reload   Home   Search   Favorites   Print   Security   Stop

Bookmarks   Netsite: http://www.beeb.com/

Inrernet shopping from the BBC

beeb.com

Go shopping

Motoring
Gardening
Travel
Homes
Electrical
Tickets
Books
CDs
Video
Full directory

Need help?

Trust beeb.com
Privacy policy
Shopping online
Contact us

Get advice   Use one of our shopping guides

BBC   BBC   BBC   BBC
music   homes   Gardeners'   H◆LIDAY
                                World

Elsewhere in beeb.com

freebeeb.net
internet access

Document Done

Looking to the Future

Today, most people who are connected to the Internet are accessing it via computer. In the future, more and more people will use other devices to go online. WAP (Wireless Application Protocol) phones are special mobile phones with an Internet connection; digital television sets and games consoles such as Sega Dreamcast will also allow you Internet access. Imagine being able to shop on your television while you are watching your favourite TV programme. For example, if you are watching Gardeners' World and would like to buy the plant they are showing, you will be able to buy it there and then because your television will be connected to the Internet.

You could even have your whole house 'web enabled', with all your household electrical appliances – such as the refrigerator and the microwave – having access to the Internet. Your refrigerator or dustbin could then update the shopping list that you have with your supermarket so that it adds goods to your shopping list if you have run out of them. Or your washing machine could talk to its manufacturer so that it will set the right wash programme for the clothes you are about to put in the wash. The possibilities are endless.

There will always be a need for shops in our towns and villages. But the Internet and Internet shopping are here to stay and will eventually make all our lives easier.

The Internet has been called the most important breakthrough in human history since we learned how to use language. It is due to the skill and hard work of many men and women that we are now able to shop on the Internet, and it is thanks to pioneering organisations such as beeb.com that we can embark on a journey along this electronic Silk Road. You may be sure it will be every bit as colourful and exciting as the original!

A WAP phone

Short Glossary

Banner – *An advertisement, often at the top of a web page.*

Browser – *The window through which you view the Internet. The browser appears once you have clicked on the browser icon on your screen.*

CD ROM (Compact Disc Read Only Memory) – *The shiny disk that sends information through your computer.*

Cookies – *These remind a web site of what you bought last time you visited, or any information you may have given them.*

Directory – *A list of web sites on the Internet, put together by people, not machines.*

Drop down box – *A box on the screen with a menu of information for you to click on.*

E-mail – *The means of sending electronic messages through the Internet.*

E-tailer – *An online shop.*

GIF (Graphics Interchange Format) – *A graphic piece of text, such as an icon.*

http – Hyper Text Transfer Protocol – *The strings of letters that let computers identify which web site you are looking for.*

Icon – *A small graphic shape on your computer screen.*

Information Superhighway – *An old-fashioned way of describing the Web.*

Internet (or 'Net') – *The network that allows one computer to send information to another.*

ISP (Internet Service Provider) – *The company that provides you with access to the Internet.*

JPEG (Joint Photographic Experts Group) – *A photograph that appears quickly and easily on your screen.*

Short Glossary – continued

Links – *Click on these to take you to a different page, or web site, on the Web.*

Modem – *The device that lets us send words, numbers or pictures between computers through wires.*

Mouse – *The device that lets us move the arrow on the computer screen, and that allows us to click on the information we want.*

Online – *When we are using the Internet we are online.*

PC – *A Personal Computer like the ones in our homes or business.*

Portals – *These are sites that link you to a range of other sites, often e-tailers.*

Return Key – *The button on your keyboard with the arrow pointing down and to the left. Press this and it has the same effect as clicking with the mouse.*

Search Engine – *A service that allows you to look up information on the Internet. These can be web crawlers or directories.*

Shopping basket (US = Cart) – *Click on this when you have chosen an item you wish to purchase.*

Telex – *The way that people sent written information through wires before e-mail.*

URL (Universal Resource Locator) – *An Internet address, eg. http://www.beeb.com*

WAP (Wireless Application Protocol) – *This allows you to access the Internet through a mobile phone.*

Web crawler – *An automatic way of searching for information on the Internet using key words.*

Wired – *Being on the Internet or being online.*

World Wide Web – *The network of sites on the Internet whose address begin 'http:'*